Copyright © 2023 by Ingo Blum

www.ingoblumbooks.com
published by planetOh concepts Gmbh, Cologne, Germany
www.planetohconcepts.com

All rights reserved. No part of this publication may be reproduced, distributed or transmitted in any form or by any means, including photocopying, recording, or other electronic or mechanical methods, without the prior written permission of the publisher, except in the case of brief quotations embodied in critical reviews and certain other noncommercial uses permitted by copyright law. Thanks!

Publisher`s Note:
Please note that the Portuguese and English versions of the story were written to be as close as possible. However, in some cases they may differ in order to accomodate the nuances and fluidity of each language. Author, translator, and publisher made every effort to ensure accuracy.

Illustrated by Ira Baykovska
Book layout by Emy Farella
Cover Layout by Inga Lämmlein
Translation by Tiago Gomes

First Edition 2023 - ISBN: 979-8374219258

Join my newsletter and get 5 ebooks for FREE at
bit.ly/5freebooks

Ingo Blum

Salvem o Mundo!
É o único planeta que tem Chocolate.

Save the World!
It is the only planet that has Chocolate.

Illustrated by Ira Baykovska

Bilingual
English
Portuguese

Once there was a boy.
He was a victim of a war.
He had to run away with his parents from the place he was born.

Era uma vez um menino.
Ele era uma vitima de uma guerra.
Ele teve de fugir com os seus pais do local onde nasceu.

He met a soldier who said to him, "Save the world! It's the only planet that has chocolate!" And he gave the boy some chocolate.

Pelo caminho, ele conheceu um soldado, que lhe disse:
– **Salva o mundo!** É o único planeta que tem chocolate! E deu um pouco de **chocolate** ao menino.

He came to a big city that
he did not know.

Ele chegou a uma grande cidade,
a qual não conhecia.

He went to a school
where the kids did not like him.
The boy was lonely.

Ele foi para uma escola onde as crianças não gostavam dele.
O menino sentia-se solitário.

His teacher said,
"Kindness can change the world."
It saves the world because
kindness is special.

A sua professora disse-lhe:
— A bondade consegue mudar o mundo.
Salva o mundo porque a bondade é
especial.

The boy was tired of being alone. However, while looking for a friend, he realized he was not the only boy who seemed lonely.

O menino estava cansado de sentir-se sozinho. Contudo, enquanto procurava por um amigo, ele percebeu que não era o único menino que parecia solitário.

He shared his chocolate with the other lonely boy, and they became friends. He thought, chocolate is wonderful, but friendship is sweeter.
Save the world because friends are important.

Ele partilhou um pouco de chocolate com o outro menino solitário, e ambos ficaram amigos. Ele pensou, o chocolate é maravilhoso, mas a amizade é mais doce. Salva o mundo porque os amigos são importantes.

The boy grew up.

He was a young man now.

He found a job.

O menino cresceu.

Agora, era um **jovem adulto**.

Ele encontrou um **trabalho**.

He met a woman he fell in love with.

Ele conheceu uma rapariga que amava.

He married her.
At their wedding, they had a big chocolate cake.
Chocolate was still wonderful, but not as sweet as his wife.

Ele casou com ela.
No seu casamento, eles tinham um grande bolo de chocolate. O chocolate ainda era maravilhoso, mas não tão doce quanto a sua esposa.

Eventually, he had children of his own. And he told them about the values of life. "It is love, kindness, friendship, and peace that make us happy," he said.

Eventualmente, ele teve os seus próprios filhos. E contou-lhe sobre as **doçuras da vida**.
– É o amor, a bondade, a amizade e a paz. – Disse ele.

The joy of his kids gave him happiness. He remembered the soldier's words but added to them.
Save the world, your children deserve it!

A **alegria** dos seus filhos dava-lhe felicidade.
Ele recordou-se das **palavras do soldado**, mas acrescentou.
Salva o mundo, as crianças merecem-no.

The years passed.
The boy, who was once a young man, grew older.
And so did his family.

Os anos passaram.
O menino, que tornou-se outrora num jovem adulto, **envelheceu**.
Bem como a sua família.

He saw his kids grow.

His parents die.

And the country change.

Ele viu os seus filhos **crescerem**.

Os seus **pais** morreram.

E o **país** mudou.

Then, another war came and changed everything. The boy, who was now an old man, stood at his door and saw some soldiers passing by.

Depois, outra guerra surgiu e mudou tudo. O menino, que era agora um idoso, estava à sua porta e viu alguns soldados a passar.

The old man approached one soldier and said, "Return back home, because peace shall be for everyone." And he gave the soldier some chocolate.

O idoso aproximou-se dele e disse:
— Regresso a casa, porque a **paz deve ser para todos.**
E deu um pouco de chocolate ao soldado.

PICS TO COLOR

The Sweets of Life

Love and happiness
Family and friendship
Peace and kindness

Amor e felicidade
Família e amizade
Paz e gentileza

Bilingual Children's Books

Visit me at
www.ingoblumbooks.com
www.planetohconcepts.com

Scan the QR-Code
and get 5 ebooks
FOR FREE!

bit.ly/5freebooks

Follow Ingo Blum

 ingoblumauthor

 ingosplanet

 ingosplanet

Printed in Great Britain
by Amazon